contents

introduction   4

soups and starters   10

salads   24

chicken in a pan   42

stir fries   58

grills   72

roasts and bakes   88

index   110

chicken

igloo

Published by Igloo Books Ltd
Cottage Farm
Sywell
NN6 0BJ
www.igloo-books.com

10 9 8 7 6 5 4 3 2 1

ISBN: 978 1 84817 633 1

Project Managed by R&R Publications Marketing Pty Ltd

Food Photography: R&R Photostudio (www.rrphotostudio.com.au)
Recipe Development: R&R Test Kitchen

Front cover photograph © Stockfood/Michael Visser

Printed in and manufactured in China

introduction

Chicken has always been a valuable food source. From the earliest recorded history, it has appeared on the tables of ancient Egypt, Greece, Rome and Asia.

The ancestor of the chicken of today is thought to be the Indian Jungle Fowl which was domesticated by the Indus Valley civilisation in about 2500 BC. It's not known how the bird travelled to other areas, but travel it did. The chicken has been used by almost all cultures throughout the world – each adding aspects of their culinary heritage to this versatile meat.

With this rich diversity of cultures, our repertoire of chicken dishes has expanded to new dimensions. Ethnic dishes from other countries, such as Tandoori Chicken, Chicken Cacciatore and Hawaiian Chicken, are just as popular in the world as the traditional roast chicken.

Through the pages of this book you will experience the new flavour combinations which have resulted from our culinary cultural exchange, presented in simple and quick-to-prepare recipes.

Chicken production today has made available not only the bird dressed and ready for the pot, but also each cut portioned out so you can buy as you need. Gone are the days when the favourite part of the family chicken, usually the breast, was the most popular piece.

NUTRITIONAL VALUE

Chicken is high in first class protein, which means it has of the essential amino acids. Vitamins, particularly A and the B group, are well represented, as are minerals including iron and zinc. It is a light, tender meat which makes it easy to chew and digest, so it is especially suitable for infants, children and the elderly. With the skin removed, chicken is even lower in fat, making it an ideal food for everyone.

PURCHASING AND STORAGE OF CHICKEN

Chicken can be purchased fresh or frozen, whole or in pieces. The choice is yours, depending how and when you wish to prepare and eat the chicken.

FRESH CHICKEN

- When buying fresh chicken, make it the last purchase on your shopping trip. It's advisable to take an insulated bag to place the chicken in to keep it cold on the trip home.

- On arriving home with your chicken purchase, remove it from the package (if any), rinse it and wipe it dry with a paper towel. Cover it loosely with plastic wrap and refrigerate immediately. Fresh chicken may be kept in the refrigerator for 3 days. Place it in the coldest part of the refrigerator, below 4°C/39°F.

- If chicken needs to be stored longer, it's better to buy ready frozen chicken than to buy it fresh and freeze it at home.

- If chicken pieces are to be purchased and frozen for future use, make sure they're are fresh. Wipe them dry with paper towel, then pack them flat in plastic freezer bags. Remove air by pushing it towards the opening and tape the bag closed. Label and date the packages.

FROZEN CHICKEN

- When purchasing frozen chicken, check that the packages are not torn.

- Place them in the freezer immediately you return home.

- Thaw frozen chicken thoroughly before cooking to avoid toughening the texture and to reduce the chance of undercooking. Undercooked parts can harbour food-spoiling bacteria.

- Don't refreeze thawed chicken. It is advisable to cook thawed chicken and freeze it when cooked.

- To thaw frozen chicken, remove the wrap, place it on a rack in a dish to allow the liquid to collect beneath the chicken. Don't touch it. Cover loosely with fresh plastic wrap and place it in the refrigerator for 24 hours. This is the safest way to thaw. Thawing on the kitchen bench encourages bacteria growth and should be avoided.

PREPARATION

There are simple rules for the preparation and handling of chicken. Adhering to these rules will lessen the likelihood of bacterial growth and thereby increase the quality, flavour and enjoyment of your dishes. Many of these rules apply to other perishable foods and should become a common part of your kitchen routine.

Food producers and retailers maintain high standards of quality and cleanliness so that we can buy safe and wholesome foods with confidence. Consumers need to maintain these quality and safety standards after purchase. Perishable foods, like chicken, need special attention to prevent deterioration and possible food poisoning.

The tips below should be employed to avoid bacterial growth and transfer.

SAFE FOOD HANDLING TIPS

- Wash your hands thoroughly before handling fresh chicken. Wash them again before handling other food.

- Chopping boards, knives and other utensils must be washed with hot soapy water after handling raw chicken and other raw foods to prevent cross-contamination .

- Always keep cold food at 4°C or below in a refrigerator.

- Never keep raw chicken at room temperature for longer than 1 hour, including preparation time.

- Poultry must be cooked through to the centre, not left rare. This ensures that all bacteria have been killed by the heat penetration. To test, insert a skewer into the centre of the chicken or portion – if the juice runs clear, the chicken is cooked through.

- Stuffing should be treated with special care as bacteria from raw poultry can grow in it. Stuff loosely, only two thirds full, just before cooking and remove the stuffing immediately after cooking.

- Large quantities of food should be divided into smaller portions to allow quicker cooking. This relates particularly to simmered chicken and chicken stock. Do not be afraid to place hot foods in the refrigerator – it is built to take them.

- The danger zone for bacterial growth is between 4°C and 65°C, so keep foods below or above this range. Food must not be left to stand on the kitchen bench, as room temperature is in the danger zone.

- When reheating cooked chicken, bring it to 75°C and hold it there for a few minutes.

soups and starters

Spicy Chicken Soup (Soto Ayam)

(see photograph on page 10)

1½ kg whole chicken

2 teaspoons salt

2 tablespoons chicken stock powder

100g vermicelli noodles

1 tablespoon peanut oil

2 cloves garlic, crushed

2 teaspoons root ginger, grated

1 stalk lemongrass, white part finely chopped and top part tied in a knot

1 teaspoon ground turmeric

2 teaspoons ground coriander

2 lime leaves, finely sliced

juice of 1 lime

wedges of lime to serve

GARNISHES

4 green onions, sliced

1 cup bean sprouts, trimmed

2 hard boiled eggs, quartered

2 potatoes, cooked and sliced

1 Place chicken in a large saucepan. Cover with water, add salt and bring to the boil. Reduce heat, cover and simmer for 30–35 minutes or until chicken is cooked. Remove chicken and strain liquid, reserving 6 cups. Stir in chicken stock powder. Remove skin and bones from chicken and shred chicken.

2 Cook noodles according to packet directions. Drain and set aside.

3 Heat oil in a large saucepan. Add garlic, ginger and lemongrass and cook for 1–2 minutes. Add turmeric and coriander and cook until aromatic.

4 Add reserved stock, chicken and lime leaves. Simmer for 10 minutes. Add lime juice just before serving.

5 Place noodles in serving bowls. Spoon chicken soup over noodles and top with garnishes. Serve with wedges of lime, sambal kecap

Serves 4

Bread Soup with Garlic and Eggs

(see photograph opposite)

¼ cup olive oil

6 thick slices firm bread, cut into cubes

2 onions, finely chopped

4 cloves garlic, crushed

6 cups good chicken stock

¼ cup freshly chopped coriander

4 eggs, at room temperature

1 teaspoon vinegar

salt and freshly ground black pepper

1 Heat 2 tablespoons olive oil in a frying pan. Cook bread in batches until golden. Remove and drain on paper towel.

2 Heat remaining oil in a large saucepan over medium heat. Cook onion and garlic until soft.

3 Add chicken stock and bring to the boil. Simmer for 5 minutes. Add coriander and season with salt and pepper.

4 Meanwhile fill a frying pan with 2cm water and vinegar. Bring to the boil over very low heat. Break eggs one at a time and gently place in water. Cook until whites are just cooked. Remove with a slotted spoon.

5 Spoon stock in bowls and top with bread and an egg.

Serves 4

Make a Meal of Chicken Soup

2 rashers bacon

1 onion

2 cloves garlic

1 tablespoon oil

300g can butter beans

1 litre chicken stock

2 potatoes

200g skinless, boneless chicken pieces

1 cup shelled broad beans

freshly ground black pepper

1 Derind bacon and chop into thin strips. Peel onion and chop finely. Crush, peel and chop garlic.

2 Heat oil in a large saucepan and saute onion, garlic and bacon for 5 minutes or until onion is clear. Drain beans and add to saucepan with stock. Bring to the boil. Peel potatoes and cut into 1cm cubes. Add to stock and cook for 10 minutes. Cut chicken into small pieces if large. Add chicken and broad beans to saucepan.

3 Cook for 5 minutes or until chicken is cooked. Serve hot with freshly ground black pepper.

Serves 4

Note: A substantial soup filled with chicken, something starchy like potatoes rice or pasta, and plenty of vegetables makes a complete meal in a bowl. This is delicious for a lighter style winter meal.

Old-Fashioned Chicken and Vegetable Soup

39g packet creamy vegetable soup mix

1 litre cold water

3 skinless chicken pieces

2 carrots

1 small parsnip

1 stalk celery

1 tablespoon chopped parsley

1 Mix packet of soup with water. Add chicken pieces and cook for 20 minutes. Peel or scrub carrots and parsnip. Grate coarsely. Trim celery and chop finely. Ten minutes before the end of cooking, remove chicken from soup and take flesh off bones if it hasn't already fallen off. Discard bones and return chicken to soup with prepared vegetables. Cook for 10 minutes.

2 Serve sprinkled with chopped parsley.

Serves 4

Note: We all love those comfort foods like vegetable soup with split peas and barley but few of us have the time to make such a soup from scratch. Here's a quicker substitute.

Chicken and Leek Soup with Herb Dumplings

(see photograph opposite)

4 chicken cutlets

1 onion, chopped

1 carrot, chopped

herb bundle made up of fresh tarragon, parsley and a bay leaf

6 cups hot water

60g butter

300g potatoes, peeled, diced

3 large leeks, sliced

salt and freshly ground black pepper

2 boneless skinless chicken breasts, cut into small pieces

2 teaspoons chopped fresh tarragon

¾ cup light cream

DUMPLINGS

125g plain flour

½ teaspoon bicarbonate of soda

30g fresh white breadcrumbs

50g butter

3 tablespoons chopped fresh herbs, such as tarragon, parsley or chives

1 Place the chicken, onion, carrot and bundle of herbs in a slow cooker with the hot water. Cover and cook for 2 hours on high, then strain the stock and skim off any fat. Finely chop the chicken, discarding the skin and bones.

2 Heat half of the butter in a large saucepan, add the potatoes and two-thirds of the leeks, cover and cook for 10 minutes. Transfer to the slow cooker and add 4 cups of the stock and season. Cook for 50 minutes, until vegetables have softened. Blend in a food processor or with a hand-held blender until smooth, return to the slow cooker, then stir in the cooked chicken.

3 Add the rest of the butter and the chicken breast and the remaining leek. Cook for 2 hours, adding more stock if necessary. Remove from the heat and stir in the fresh tarragon and cream. To serve, divide between 6 bowls, drain the dumplings and add 2 to each bowl.

DUMPLINGS (make while finishing the soup)

1 Mix together the flour, bicarbonate of soda, breadcrumbs, butter, herbs and seasoning. Stir in water, then shape into 12 dumplings. Cook in simmering salted water for 15 minutes.

Serves 6

Chicken and Almond Triangles

1 tablespoon olive oil

½ cup slivered almonds

1 medium onion, finely chopped

½ teaspoon salt

1 teaspoon ground cinnamon

1 teaspoon paprika

2 teaspoons ground cumin

500g minced chicken meat

2 small tomatoes, chopped

¼ cup raisins, chopped

2 tablespoons finely chopped Italian
  parsley

¼ cup dry white wine

1 packet filo pastry

vegetable oil spray

1 Heat the oil in a frying pan and sauté the almonds until pale gold in colour. Quickly remove with a slotted spoon and drain on paper towel. Add the onion and fry until soft, stir in the salt and spices and cook until aromatic. Add the minced chicken and stir-fry until almost cooked. Add the tomatoes, raisins, parsley, almonds and wine and simmer, covered, 15 minutes. Uncover and cook until the juices are absorbed. Allow to cool.

2 Thaw the pastry according to packet instructions. Count out 14 sheets, repack and refreeze the remainder. Position the pastry with the long side parallel to bench edge in front of you. Cut it into 3 x 15cm wide strips. Stack and cover with clean tea towel. Taking 2 strips at a time, spray each lightly with canola oil spray and fold in half, long side to long side. Spray the surface with oil spray.

3 Place a teaspoon of filling on the bottom end of each strips. Fold the right-hand corner over to form a triangle then fold on the straight then on the diagonal until end is reached. Repeat with remaining. Place on a tray sprayed with oil. Spray the tops of the triangles with oil and bake in a preheated moderate oven for 20–25 minutes. Serve hot as finger food.

Makes 42

Variation: 250g chicken stir-fry fried with 1 chopped onion, cooled and mixed into 250g ricotta cheese and 1 beaten egg.

Spicy Chicken Burritos

1 kg chicken stir-fry

1 tablespoon olive oil

1 large onion, finely chopped

1 clove garlic, crushed

¾ cup packaged tomato sauce of choice

½ teaspoon chilli powder

TOPPINGS

1 tub guacamole

2 large onions, thinly sliced

½ carton sour cream

340g grated tasty cheddar cheese

400g refried beans, heated (optional)

12 Mexican tortillas

1 Chop the stir-fry into smaller pieces. Heat the oil in a large frying pan. Add the onion and garlic and fry until soft. Add the chicken and stir to brown it on all sides. Stir in the sauce and the chilli powder. Simmer for 15 minutes or until chicken is cooked.

2 Prepare the toppings and place in serving dishes. Heat the tortillas by the method on the pack. The preferred method is to heat a large frying pan and place in a tortilla. Heat the for 40 seconds each side, long enough to roast slightly. Remove and place in a clean towel and cover. Heat remainder and stack in the towel. Serve in the towel in a basket.

3 Invite each guest to make their own burrito by placing chicken mixture on the tortilla and adding their choice of toppings. Roll the buritto and enjoy.

Makes 12

No-Fuss Chicken Party Sticks

1 kg chicken tenderloins

salt and pepper

1⅓ kg packet frozen puff pastry

1 quantity spicy satay sauce or sweet chilli sauce

1 tablespoon poppy seeds

or sesame seeds

SPICY SATAY SAUCE

¾ cup peanut butter

¾ cup water

2 tablespoons brown sugar

⅛ teaspoon chilli powder, or to taste

1 tablespoon soy sauce

1 tablespoon grated onion

2 tablespoons toasted sesame seeds

32 bamboo skewers, soaked

1 Sprinkle the salt and pepper over the tenderlions. Cut a sheet of thawed pastry into 4 squares. Place a tenderloin on each square and add a dash of sauce. Roll up either on the straight or on the diagonal, leaving the ends open. Place seam-side down on a flat oven tray and glaze with milk or egg wash. Sprinkle with poppy seeds or sesame seeds.

2 Bake in a preheated moderate 180°C oven for 25–30 minutes. Serve hot as finger food with the same sauce used as a dipping sauce.

3 Mix all the satay sauce ingredients together in a saucepan, heat to a simmer. Keep on the heat for 5 minutes and allow to cool.

Makes 32

Lavash Rolls

vegetable oil spray

1 kg chicken tenderloins

8 pieces lavash flat bread

1¼ cups mayonnaise

1 small lettuce, shredded

½ bunch green onions, chopped

4 tomatoes, sliced

1 tub hummus

2 tablespoons lemon juice

salt and pepper

1 Spray a heated non-stick pan or griddle plate with oil spray and cook the tenderloins for 2 minutes on each side.

2 Place each lavash sheet on a work surface. Spread lightly with mayonnaise. Sprinkle with lettuce leaving the bottom 4cm uncovered. Sprinkle green onions over the lettuce and place on tomato slices. Place 3–4 tenderloins down the centre and drizzle with a little hummus thinned with lemon juice.

3 Turn up the bottom edge to hold in the filling and roll from the side into a tight roll. Wrap the bottom half in greaseproof paper or foil and serve.

Serves 8

Note: Quantities given are for 8 rolls. Make adjustments for number required. Other salad vegetables and fruit may be used according to preference, eg: avocado, grated carrot, celery, pineapple, nuts, etc.

Chicken Rolls with Orange Currant Sauce

2 teaspoons grated orange zest

4 strips thinly peeled orange zest, cut into thin strips (julienne)

juice of 3 oranges

1 small onion, finely chopped and fried in a little butter

¼ cup fresh breadcrumbs

2 tablespoons currants

1 kg chicken thigh fillets

salt and pepper

2 ginger nut biscuits, finely crushed

2 tablespoons brandy

1 Mix together the grated orange zest, 2 tablespoons of the orange juice, the fried onions and the breadcrumbs. Flatten chicken thigh fillets with a meat mallet, smooth side down, and sprinkle with salt and pepper. Place a teaspoon of filling onto each fillet, pressing on well. Roll up and secure with a toothpick.

2 Heat butter or oil in a heavy-based frying pan and brown on all sides. Reduce heat and add remaining orange juice, scraping up any browned juices with the back of a spoon. Add currants and a pinch of salt and pepper. Cover and simmer for 20 minutes, until chicken rolls are tender. Remove rolls to a warm serving platter and, keep hot.

3 To the pan juices add the crushed ginger nut biscuits. Stir over low heat until thickened. If a thinner consistency is desired, add extra orange juice or water. Pour over chicken rolls and garnish with blanched julienne orange zest.

Serves 6

salads

Tossed Greens and Chicken with Blue Cheese Dressing

(see photograph on page 24)

1 bunch rocket

1 coral lettuce

1 mignonette lettuce

1 red apple, cored, thinly sliced, splashed with lemon juice

60g pale walnut pieces

2 poached chicken breasts

DRESSING

⅓ cup olive oil

2 tablespoons white wine vinegar

1 tablespoon lemon juice

¼ teaspoon sugar

1 tablespoon Dijon mustard

30g blue-vein cheese, crumbled

pinch cayenne

60g extra blue-vein cheese for topping

1 Wash the greens, drain and shake in a tea towel to dry. Arrange on 4 individual plates with apple slices and half the pieces.

2 Cut the chicken into slices and arrange with the salad greens. Whisk the dressing ingredients together and pour over each salad. Sprinkle the top with remaining walnut pieces and extra crumbled blue-vein cheese. Serve as an entrée or luncheon dish.

Serves 4–5

Chicken Waldorf

(see photograph opposite)

400g chicken breast fillets, poached

2 red apples

1 tablespoon lemon juice

2 sticks celery, diced

60g blond walnuts, coarsely chopped

½ cup mayonnaise

1 lettuce, separated into cups, washed and crisped

1 Poach the chicken breasts (see tip), and cool. Cut into 1cm cubes. Wash the apples well, leave the skin on and cut into 1cm cubes. Sprinkle with the lemon juice.

2 Toss the chicken, apples, celery and walnuts together. Add the mayonnaise and gently toss through.

3 Spoon into the lettuce cups and serve as an entrée or light lunch, or line a salad bowl with lettuce leaves and pile the salad into the centre and serve for a buffet.

Serves 6

Note: To poach the chicken: Cover the fillets with hot water, add a little salt, a small onion, chopped, a piece of celery and a carrot. Simmer for 20–25 minutes until tender. Remove the chicken to cool. Strain the stock, it can be reserved for future use. Discard the vegetables.

Asian Chicken and Kaffir Lime Salad

400g skinless chicken breast fillets

4 kaffir lime leaves, finely shredded

1 lime, sliced

125g Chinese (mung bean) vermicelli

250g green beans, halved

1 cup fresh coriander leaves

1 cup fresh Thai basil leaves, shredded

4 green onions, thinly sliced

2 tablespoons fried French shallots

DRESSING

2 tablespoons fish sauce

2 tablespoons lime juice

2 tablespoons palm sugar, grated

1 Put the chicken in a large, deep fry pan, add the kaffir lime leaves and lime slices and cover with water. Bring to the boil. Reduce the heat to a very slow simmer and poach the chicken for 15 minutes or until tender. Drain the chicken, reserving ¼ cup of the liquid. Allow the chicken to cool slightly then shred finely using your fingers.

2 While the chicken is cooking, put the vermicelli in a bowl and cover with boiling water. Allow to stand for 5–10 minutes or until tender, then drain well. Cook the beans until tender then drain.

3 Put the chicken, vermicelli, coriander, basil, beans, green onions and shallots into a bowl and toss to combine.

4 To make the dressing, put the reserved cooking liquid, fish sauce, lime juice and palm sugar in a jug and whisk well. Pour over the salad and toss to combine.

Serves 4

Party Avocado and Chicken Salad

1 kg chicken breast fillets

3 avocados

1 tablespoon lemon juice

2 sticks celery, thinly sliced

60g slivered almonds, toasted

½ green capsicum cut into slices

400g can mango slices, drained
  (or fresh mango in season)

1 cucumber

lettuce to serve

DRESSING

1 cup thickened cream, whipped

½ cup mayonnaise

½ grated nutmeg

1 teaspoon paprika

salt and pepper

1 Poach the chicken as per tip below, cool then cut into large dice 1½cm–2½ cm cubes. Peel and slice the avocado and sprinkle with lemon juice.

2 Combine the chicken, celery, almonds, capsicum and most of the avocado, mango slices and cucumber.

3 Mix the dressing ingredients together, pour over the salad and toss gently. Arrange the lettuce leaves on a shallow platter; pile on the chicken mixture. Garnish with the reserved avocado, mango and cucumber.

Serves 10–20

Note: To poach the chicken: Cover the fillets with hot water, add a little salt, a small onion, chopped, a piece of celery and a carrot. Simmer for 20–25 minutes until tender. Remove the chicken to cool. Strain the stock, it can be reserved for future use. Discard the vegetables.

Chicken Caesar Salad

(see photograph opposite)

2 chicken breast fillets

1 clove garlic, crushed

salt and pepper

2 teaspoons olive oil

1 tablespoon lemon juice

1 Romaine lettuce

DRESSING

2 anchovy fillets

4 tablespoons olive oil

2½ tablespoons lemon juice

½ teaspoon salt

¼ teaspoon pepper

1 coddled egg

pinch of dry mustard

1 teaspoon Worcestershire sauce

¼ cup grated Parmesan cheese

1 cup garlic croutons

shaved Parmesan cheese for garnish

1 Trim the chicken fillets. Mix together the garlic, salt, pepper, oil and lemon juice, cover and marinate the chicken for 30 minutes in the refrigerator. Heat grill or chargrill until hot. Sear the fillets 1 minute on each side, then cook for 3 minutes each side. Remove and rest for 5 minutes before cutting into ½cm slices on the diagonal.

2 Separate the leaves of the lettuce, discard outer leaves and wash well. Drain and shake dry in a clean tea towel. Cut the greener leaves into bite-sized pieces and leave the pale inner leaves whole. Cover and place in the refrigerator until ready for use.

3 Place the anchovy fillets in base of the salad bowl and mash with the back of a fork while the oil is being added. Gradually add the lemon juice while beating and sprinkle in the salt and pepper. Break in the coddled egg, scraping the set white from inside the shell and lightly stir. Add the mustard and Worcestershire sauce.

4 Add the lettuce leaves; toss to coat lightly with dressing while sprinkling over the grated Parmesan cheese. Toss in the chicken and croutons. Rearrange the whole leaves to stand upright and garnish with the shaved Parmesan cheese. Serve immediately.

Serves 5

To coddle an egg: Bring the egg to room temperature. Boil water in a small saucepan and when it reaches the boil, turn the heat off and immediately lower in the egg. Stand for 1 minute in the water. If the egg is cold from refrigerator, allow 1½ minutes.

To make croutons: Use unsliced day-old white bread. Cut slices 1½cm thick, remove crusts and cut into 1½cm cubes. Peel 2 cloves of garlic and cut them in half. Add enough oil to be 5mm deep in the frying pan, add the garlic and heat. Remove garlic when golden; add the bread cubes, stir and toss as they fry to golden colour. Remove quickly from the pan and drain on paper towels.

To joint a chicken: Remove the leg and thigh at the joint. Separate the leg and thigh cutting through the joint. Remove the wings at the joint. Cut the breast from the backbone along the fine rib bones on each side. Cut through the centre breast bone. Cut each breast into 2 pieces.

Curried Chicken Salad

1 large, ready cooked barbecued chicken

2 sticks celery, finely chopped

6 green onions, sliced

⅓ cup raisins, soaked

60g slivered almonds, toasted

200g mixed salad greens, washed and crisped

assorted fresh fruits to garnish

toasted shredded coconut to garnish

DRESSING

½ cup mayonnaise

½ cup low-fat yoghurt

3 tablespoons sweet mango chutney

1 tablespoon mild curry paste

2 tablespoons lemon juice

2 teaspoons freshly grated

lemon zest

1 Remove the chicken meat from the bones and cut into bite-size pieces. Toss with the celery, green onions, raisins and almonds.

2 Place all dressing ingredients in a bowl and whisk until smooth.

3 Pour the dressing over the chicken and toss to mix through. Cover and chill for 2 hours or more. Line a platter or individual plates with salad greens and pile on the chicken mixture. Garnish with fruits and coconut.

Serves 8

Note: Quantities given are for 8 rolls. Make adjustments for number required. Other salad vegetables and fruit may be used according to preference, eg: avocado, grated carrot, celery, pineapple, nuts, etc.

Tropical Chicken Salad

2 large skinless chicken breast fillets

1 Lebanese cucumber, diced

1 cup diced fresh or unsweetened
canned pineapple

½ cup diced pawpaw

¼ cup unsalted cashews

2 green onions, sliced diagonally

2 tablespoons chopped fresh coriander

2 tablespoons chopped fresh mint

CHILLI AND LIME DRESSING

1 fresh red chilli, thinly sliced

finely grated zest of 1 lime

juice of 2 limes

1 tablespoon fish sauce

1 tablespoon rice wine vinegar

½ teaspoon sesame oil

1   Preheat the barbecue to a high heat.

2   Cook the chicken on the barbecue grill for 4–5 minutes each side or until cooked through. Alternatively, place the chicken in a frying pan and pour water or a mixture of water and wine to cover it. Cover. Bring to simmering. Poach for 10 minutes or until the chicken is cooked. Cool. Cut into thin strips.

3   Place the chicken, cucumber, pineapple, pawpaw, cashews, green onions, coriander and mint in a bowl. Toss to combine.

4   To make the dressing, place the chilli, lime zest and juice, fish sauce, vinegar and oil in a screwtop jar. Shake to combine. Drizzle the dressing over the salad. Toss. Cover. Refrigerate for at least 15 minutes before serving – this allows the flavours to develop.

Serves 4

Note: If you're in a hurry, buy a cooked chicken from a store that does not smother the bird in fat before or during cooking.

Warm Salad of Mustard-Glazed Chicken with Red Wine Vinaigrette

3 tablespoons mustard seeds

3 tablespoons malt vinegar

2 tablespoons honey

1 tablespoon molasses

1 tablespoon brown sugar

½ cup olive oil

4 tablespoons French mustard

2 cloves garlic, minced

½ cup boiling water

8 skinless chicken breast fillets

2 tablespoons red or white wine vinegar

2 tablespoons olive oil

salt and pepper to taste

300g assorted baby lettuce leaves, well washed and dried

300g baby spinach leaves, well washed and dried

1 bunch green onions, sliced on the diagonal

1 bunch chives, chopped

1 To make the marinade, grind two tablespoons of the mustard seeds into powder, then mix with the malt vinegar, honey molasses, brown sugar, olive oil, French mustard, garlic and boiling water. Whisk well until the mixture is thick and smooth.

2 Reserve 4 tablespoons of marinade for later use. Lay the chicken in a flat glass dish and pour the remaining marinade over. Turn the chicken so that both sides are covered in the marinade and chill for at least 4 hours.

3 Remove the chicken from the marinade, making sure that each piece of chicken has a good coating of the marinade. Place in an ovenproof baking dish or on an oven tray and bake at 210°C for 20–25 minutes, until cooked through.

4 Meanwhile, transfer the reserved marinade to a saucepan and bring to the boil. Simmer for 5 minutes then remove from the heat. Remove the chicken from the oven and keep warm.

5 Make a dressing with the red or white wine vinegar and olive oil with salt and pepper to taste and a little of the reserved warm marinade. Whisk well. Toss some dressing through the mixed lettuce and spinach leaves just to coat them. Add the green onions and chives and toss again.

6 To serve, arrange the salad leaves on plates then top each mound of salad with a chicken breast, sliced on the diagonal. Drizzle around a little remaining warm marinade.

Serves 8

Marinated Chicken Salad

2 cups vegetable oil

500g chicken stir-fry

½ cup seasoned flour

¼ cup orange juice

¼ cup olive oil

1 tablespoon mint, chopped

½ teaspoon salt

freshly ground black pepper

1 avocado, sliced

400g can apricot halves

1 punnet snow pea sprouts

1 Heat the oil in a deep frying pan. Dip the stir-fry strips in the flour, a few at a time, and deep-fry in the hot oil until cooked and golden in colour. Drain on absorbent paper, then place in a glass bowl.

2 Combine the orange juice, oil, mint, salt and pepper in a screw-top jar and shake well. Pour over the chicken strips and refrigerate for at least 30 minutes.

3 Slice the avocado and drain the apricot halves, reserving two tablespoons of juice from the can. Arrange the snow pea sprouts on individual plates. Top with the chicken strips, avocado pieces and apricot halves. Add 1–2 teaspoons of juice to the remaining marinade and drizzle over the salad. Serve as an entrée or as a luncheon dish with crusty bread.

Serves 6–8

Chicken and Pawpaw Salad

½ pawpaw

2 kiwifruit

6 slices stale toast bread

vegetable oil spray

small salad greens

3 cups cooked boneless chicken

FOR ADULTS

¼ cup oil

2 tablespoons white vinegar

½ teaspoon prepared mustard

1 Deseed pawpaw. Peel and cut into cubes. Peel kiwifruit and cut into cubes. Cut crusts from bread. Spray each side with oil. Place on a baking tray. Grill until lightly golden. Turn bread and cut into cubes. Grill until bread is golden and crisp.

2 Toss salad greens with chicken, pawpaw, kiwifruit and bread croutons. Serve drizzled with dressing.

FOR KIDS

1 Any dressing they'll eat, or serve the salad undressed

FOR ADULTS

1 Mix oil, vinegar and mustard together.

Serves 4–6

Note: Raw vegetables always seem to be more popular with kids for some reason. I introduced main meal salads to my kids by making homemade croutons which they still love.

Festive Chicken Salad

1½ kg chicken, roasted

1 bunch English spinach

1 coral lettuce

1 radicchio lettuce

6 slices of bread

2 tablespoons olive oil

4 rashers bacon

1 can mango slices or 1 fresh mango, sliced

2 small Spanish onions, thinly sliced

2 avocados, peeled and sliced

DRESSING

½ cup olive oil

¼ cup vinegar

1 teaspoon Dijon mustard

1 teaspoon sugar

1 teaspoon fresh thyme

1 teaspoon lemon zest

GARNISH

nasturtium flowers

DRESSING

1   Combine all dressing ingredients together in a screw topped jar and shake well. Stand 30 minutes to concentrate flavour.

SALAD

1   Wash the spinach and lettuce, drain well, place in a clean kitchen towel and refrigerate for 1 hour to crisp. Tear into bite sized pieces.

2   Remove crusts from bread, cut into small dice. Fry until golden and crisp in hot oil. Drain on paper towels.

3   Dice the bacon and fry until crisp.

4   Drain the mango slices, cut each in half lengthwise or peel and slice the fresh mango into strips.

5   Remove breast from chicken, discard skin and cut into strips. Remove leg and thigh portions, discard skin and slice thinly.

6   Toss together spinach, lettuce, onion slices, croutons and bacon. Toss well with half of the dressing. Spread onto a large tray or serving platter then arrange half of the chicken slices on top, leaving a border of salad. Place a row of avocado slices over the chicken, indenting to show some chicken, then more chicken slices followed by mango. Top with a small pile of chicken. Drizzle remaining dressing over the layers and garnish top with nasturtium flowers.

Serves 15

Crunchy Chicken and Potato Salad

500g potatoes, medium-sized

water to cover

1 teaspoon salt

1 tablespoon olive oil

1 large onion, finely chopped

1 clove garlic, crushed

200g minced chicken meat

1 tablespoon lemon juice

salt and pepper to taste

1 cup mayonnaise

1 small red chilli, seeded and finely chopped (optional)

dill feathers to garnish

small lettuce leaves to garnish

1 Wash and peel the potatoes and cut each into 4–6 wedges. Place in boiling water to cover, add salt and cook for 20 minutes. Drain and cool.

2 Heat the oil in a large frying pan, add the onion and garlic and fry until the onion is soft. Stir in the minced chicken and brown while stirring continuously. This will take about 15 minutes. Add the lemon juice and stir up the cooked pan juices. When the minced chicken is brown and crumbly, season with a little salt and pepper, remove from the heat and cool.

3 Mix the cooled potatoes and two thirds of the minced chicken and the mayonnaise together gently, tossing in the chilli. Pile into a clean salad bowl or platter and pile ing the remaining minced chicken in a pile on the top. Garnish with dill feathers and surround with small lettuce leaves if desired. Serve as a luncheon salad or buffet item.

Serves 6

Chicken and Endive Salad with Creamy Dressing

1 slender French bread stick (baguette)

1 clove garlic, crushed

2 tablespoons oil

1 bunch curly endive, washed and drained dry

4 green onions, sliced

225g can mandarin segments, drained (juice reserved)

250g chicken tenderloins

DRESSING

1 cup coleslaw dressing

1 teaspoon Dijon mustard

1 Cut the bread stick into ½cm slices. Mix the garlic and oil together and brush onto the bread slices. Place on a tray in a moderate oven 170°C and cook until crisp and golden. Break the endive into 5cm pieces; mix with the green onions and mandarin segments.

2 Cook the tenderloins in a lightly greased non-stick pan for 2 minutes each side.

3 Mound the croutons and endive salad onto individual serving plates and arrange the chicken on top. Mix the dressing ingredients together and pour on the top, allowing it to run down the sides. Serve as an entrée.

Serves 4

chicken
in a pan

Hawaiian Poached Chicken

(see photograph on page 42)

1⅓ kg fresh chicken

½ teaspoon each salt and pepper

1 teaspoon paprika

2 tablespoons oil

1 large onion, chopped

1 clove garlic, crushed

¼ cup water

1 tablespoon Worcestershire sauce

2 teaspoons sweet chilli sauce

¼ cup apple cider vinegar

1½ tablespoons brown sugar

½ medium, fresh pineapple, peeled and diced

1 green capsicum, seeded and cut into thin strips

1 red capsicum, seeded and cut into thin strips

1 tablespoon rum (optional)

1½ tablespoon cornflour

1½ tablespoon water

boiled rice to serve

1 Joint the chicken into serving pieces as per tip below. Season with salt, pepper and paprika. Heat the oil in a large saucepan. Add the chicken pieces, a few at a time, and brown on all sides. Remove to a plate lined with kitchen paper as they brown.

2 Add the onion and garlic to the saucepan and cook, stirring for 2 minutes. Return the chicken to the saucepan. Combine the water, the 2 sauces, the vinegar and the sugar and pour over the chicken. Add the pineapple and capsicums. Simmer for 25–30 minutes until chicken is tender.

3 Warm and flame the rum and pour into the chicken. Blend the cornflour and water together, add to the chicken and stir through. Allow to simmer until it thickens. Increase the heat until it boils then turn off immediately. Serve with boiled rice.

Serves 6

Note: To joint a chicken. Remove the leg and thigh at the joint. Separate the leg and thigh cutting through the joint. Remove the wings at the joint. Cut the breast from the backbone along the fine rib bones on each side. Cut through the centre breast bone. Cut each breast into 2 pieces.

Date and Lemon Chicken Casserole

(see photograph opposite)

1 kg chicken pieces

2 cloves garlic

1 onion

2 teaspoons ground cumin

1 teaspoon paprika

1 cup chopped dates

1 lemon

1 teaspoon brown sugar

1 teaspoon salt

freshly ground black pepper

¼ cup wine vinegar

2 cups chicken stock

1 Brown chicken pieces in a hot pan, turning often for 5 minutes. Place in a casserole dish. Crush, peel and roughly chop garlic. Peel onion and slice finely. Scatter onion, garlic, cumin and paprika over chicken with dates. Thinly peel lemon and cut rind into thin strips. Add to casserole with sugar, salt, pepper, vinegar and chicken stock.

2 Cover and bake at 180°C for 1½ to 2 hours. Serve with couscous or rice and green olives.

Serves 4–6

Tandoori Chicken Pockets

2 teaspoons vegetable oil

1 small onion, finely chopped

1 kg chicken stir-fry, chopped to smaller pieces

½ teaspoon salt

2 teaspoons tandoori curry paste

1 tablespoon lemon juice

1 tablespoon water

1 packet white or wholemeal pita bread pockets

3 cups shredded lettuce

2½ cups natural yoghurt

1 Heat the oil in a small pan, add the onion and fry until soft. Sprinkle the chicken with salt and fry until almost cooked. Stir in the curry paste, cook a little, then add the lemon juice and water. Allow to simmer until most of the liquid has evaporated. Stir occasionally.

2 Cut pita bread in half and open the pocket. Place the lettuce in the base of the pocket and fill with the curried chicken. Add a tablespoon of yoghurt on top. Serve immediately.

Makes 12

Note: For extra flavour, serve with a spoonful of your favourite chutney.

Lentil Chicken Marsala Casserole

500g skinned and boned chicken thighs

6 silverbeet leaves

½ cup brown lentils

285g jar tikka marsala curry sauce

1 cup boiling water

1   Cut chicken thighs in half lengthwise. Place in casserole dish. Wash silverbeet and slice finely. Place over chicken. Scatter lentils over. Mix tikka marsala sauce and boiling water together. Pour over chicken mixture.

2   Bake, covered, at 180°C for 1 hour. Uncover and cook for a further 15 minutes. Serve with sliced banana, coconut and chutney.

Serves 4

Note: Make your own chicken stock by cooking up chicken bones or a chicken carcass with water, celery, carrot, onion and a bouquet garni. Do this when you have time and freeze the stock in usable quantities for later use.

Chicken and Apricot Tagine

8 skinless, boneless chicken thighs

1 onion

2 cloves garlic

3 tablespoons oil

2 teaspoons ground ginger

1 teaspoon ground cinnamon

1 teaspoon ground paprika

1 cup pitted prunes

1 cup dried apricots

¼ cup honey

1 cup chicken stock

1 teaspoon ground coriander

1 teaspoon grated orange rind

TO SERVE

couscous

toasted almonds

chopped fresh coriander

1 Cut chicken into quarters. Place in a casserole dish. Peel onion and chop roughly. Crush, peel and chop garlic.

2 Heat oil in a frying pan and saute onion, garlic, ginger, cinnamon and paprika until onion is just softening. Add to chicken with prunes, apricots, honey, chicken stock, coriander and orange rind.

3 Bake at 160°C for 1 hour. Serve over couscous topped with almonds and coriander.

Serves 6

Note: Make this ahead of time and keep in the refrigerator for 1 to 2 days. Alternatively, freeze until ready to use. Thaw in the refrigerator and reheat thoroughly.

Apple, Chicken and Mushroom Casserole

8 chicken drumsticks

1 onion

2 apples

37g mushroom soup mix

1 teaspoon dried thyme

2 teaspoons wholegrain mustard

1½ cups water

1 cup natural unsweetened yoghurt

8 mushrooms

salt

pepper

1 Remove skin from chicken. Peel onion and slice finely. Peel apples, core and dice. Place chicken, onion and apple in a casserole dish with the mushroom soup mix, thyme, mustard and water. Place a tight-fitting lid on top.

2 Bake at 180°C for 1 hour or until chicken is tender when pierced with a fork.

3 Stir in yoghurt. Clean mushrooms and cut in half. Mix through casseroled chicken mixture. Bake for a further 10 minutes. Season with salt and pepper.

Serves 4

Chicken Wings Moroccan Style

2 tablespoons canola oil

1 kg chicken wings

1 large onion, finely chopped

1 clove garlic, crushed

1½ teaspoon chopped fresh ginger

½ teaspoon ground turmeric

½ teaspoon cumin

½ cinnamon stick

¼ cup cider vinegar

2 cups apricot nectar

salt and pepper

90g dried prunes, pitted

90g dried apricots

1 tablespoon honey

¼ cup lemon juice

steamed couscous or rice to serve

1 Heat the oil in a wide-based saucepan or lidded skillet. Add the chicken wings, a few at a time, and brown lightly on both sides. Remove to a plate as they brown.

2 Add the onion and fry for 2 minutes. Stir in the garlic, ginger and spices, cook while stirring for 1 minute, return the chicken to the pan, stir and turn the wings to coat with spices. Add the vinegar and apricot nectar and season to taste. Cover and simmer for 25 minutes.

3 Add the prunes, apricots, honey and lemon juice. Cover and simmer for 10 minutes and then remove lid and simmer uncovered for 5 minutes. If a thicker sauce is desired, remove the wings and fruit to a serving platter, increase the heat and boil until the sauce reduces and thickens, stirring occasionally. Pour the sauce over the wings. Serve immediately with steamed couscous or rice.

Serves 3–4

Chicken Paprika

8 chicken pieces

¼ cup flour

salt

pepper

1 chicken stock cube

1 tablespoon paprika

3 tablespoons oil

1 onion

125g mushrooms

410g can tomato puree

¼ cup low-fat sour cream

1 tablespoon chopped parsley

1 Remove skin from chicken and discard. Mix flour, salt, pepper, crumbled stock cube and paprika together in a plastic bag. Toss chicken in this.

2 Heat oil in a large saucepan. Brown chicken in oil. Peel and chop onion. Add to saucepan and cook for 3 to 5 minutes. Wipe mushrooms, trim and slice. Add mushrooms and tomato puree to saucepan. Cover and simmer for 45 to 50 minutes, or until chicken is cooked.

3 Garnish with sour cream and chopped parsley.

Serves 4–6

Risotto of Indian Spiced Chicken with Chickpeas

3 cloves garlic, crushed

2 teaspoons ground cumin

2 teaspoons paprika

2 teaspoons ground coriander

1 tablespoon garam masala

1 teaspoon ground ginger

3 tablespoons mango or apricot chutney

juice and zest of 1 orange

4 tablespoons olive oil

4 boneless, skinless thigh fillets cut into strips, or 12 'winglets'

1 tablespoon ghee

1 bunch green onions, trimmed and chopped

400g arborio rice

4 cups vegetable stock

400g can chickpeas, drained and rinsed

2 handfuls baby spinach, washed

125g sultanas

2 tablespoons yoghurt, optional

2 tablespoons fresh mint, chopped

salt and freshly ground black pepper

1125g toasted almonds

1 In a glass jug, mix together the garlic, cumin, paprika, coriander, Garam Marsala, ginger, chutney, orange juice and zest and oil. Mix very well then pour over the chicken in a non-reactive baking dish (glass or ceramic) and allow to marinate for 6 hours overnight.

2 In a saucepan, heat the ghee and add half the green onions and cook gently until softened. Remove the chicken from the marinade and add to the green onions, cooking until the chicken begins to change colour, about 3 minutes.

3 Remove the chicken from the pan, add the rice and begin adding the stock, half a cup at a time and allowing each to be absorbed before the next quantity of stock is added. When adding the last of the stock, add the chickpeas, baby spinach and sultanas and mix vigorously to incorporate. When the liquid has been absorbed, remove the saucepan from the heat and add the remaining green onions, yoghurt, fresh mint and salt and pepper to taste. Serve immediately, garnished with the almonds.

Serves 6

Note: The aromatic spices that marinate the chicken create delicious musky flavours that permeate the rice. The chicken will benefit from being marinated for at least 6 hours, but if time is scarce 1–2 hours will do.

Chicken Breasts with Shiitake Mushrooms

2 tablespoons groundnut oil

1 onion, chopped

5cm piece fresh root ginger, finely chopped

200g shiitake mushrooms, stems removed and caps sliced

145g baby button mushrooms

2 tablespoons dark soy sauce

1 cup chicken stock

1 cup white wine

340g patty pan squash, halved, or zucchini, trimmed and sliced

6 skinless boneless chicken breasts

chopped fresh coriander to garnish

1 Preheat the oven to 230°C. Heat 1 tablespoon of the oil in a large, heavy-based saucepan, add the onion and the ginger and fry for 5 minutes or until the onion has softened. Add the shiitake and button mushrooms and the soy sauce and cook for a further 4–5 minutes, until the mushrooms have softened.

2 Stir in the stock and wine, bring to the boil, then simmer for 10 minutes. Add the squash or zucchini and cook for a further 5 minutes or until tender.

3 Meanwhile, make 3 slashes in each chicken breast, using a sharp knife. Heat the remaining oil in a large, heavy-based frying pan, add the chicken and fry for 2–3 minutes each side to brown.

4 Transfer the chicken to an ovenproof dish and spoon over the mushroom mixture. Bake for 15–20 minutes, until the chicken is cooked through. Sprinkle with coriander just before serving.

Serves 6

Note: Shiitake mushrooms, soy sauce and fresh ginger give this dish an oriental flavour. It's great with plain boiled rice or Chinese noodles and some stir-fried green vegetables.

Italian Chicken in a Pan

6 boneless, skinless
chicken breast fillets

seasoned flour

1 egg, beaten

dried breadcrumbs

¼ cup vegetable oil

2 cups bottled tomato pasta sauce

6 slices prosciutto or ham

6 slices mozzarella cheese

6 sprigs fresh sage

1 Place the chicken between sheets of greaseproof paper and pound lightly to flatten. Dust with the flour, then dip in the egg and finally coat with the breadcrumbs. Place on a plate lined with plastic food wrap and refrigerate for 15 minutes.

2 Heat the oil in a large frying pan over a medium heat, add the chicken and cook for 2–3 minutes each side or until golden. Remove from the pan and set aside.

3 Add the pasta sauce to the pan and cook over a medium heat, stirring, for 4–5 minutes or until hot. Place the chicken in a single layer on top of the sauce, then top each fillet with a slice of prosciutto or ham, a slice of cheese and a sprig of sage. Cover and simmer for 5 minutes or until the chicken is cooked through and the cheese melts. Serve immediately.

Serves 6

Chicken Rolls with an Indonesian Flavour

1 kg chicken thigh fillets

300g Redang curry sauce

2 bananas

toothpicks

2 tablespoons vegetable oil

½ cup water

¾ cup coconut milk

1 small, fresh pineapple, peeled, and
thinly sliced

freshly ground black pepper

2 tablespoons shredded coconut,
toasted

steamed rice to serve

1 Open out the fillets on a large chopping board. Flatten with a meat mallet to an even thinness. Spread each with a teaspoon of Rendang curry sauce.

2 Peel the bananas and slit them in half lengthwise then cut them in half to make 4 pieces. Place a piece of banana in centre of each fillet and form into a roll. Fasten with a toothpick. Heat the oil in a wide-based saucepan and brown the rolls on all sides, a few at a time, removing them to a plate as they brown. Drain all the oil from the saucepan.

3 To the same saucepan, add the Rendang curry sauce and the water. Bring to the boil, reduce the heat to a simmer and place in the chicken rolls. Cover and simmer 35 minutes, turning the rolls once during cooking.

4 Remove the rolls to a heated platter and keep hot. If the sauce is thin, increase the heat and reduce the sauce to a thicker consistency. Reduce the heat and stir in the coconut milk and simmer for 2 minutes. Return the rolls to the saucepan to reheat.

5 Saute the pineapple rings in a little butter until lightly coloured and grind over some black pepper. Arrange 1–2 slices of pineapple and a chicken roll on each plate, spoon the sauce over the roll and sprinkle with a little toasted coconut. Serve with steamed rice.

Serves 4

stir-fries

Easy Chicken Stir-Fry

(see photograph on page 58)

300g chicken breast fillets

1 tablespoon sweet chilli sauce

1 tablespoon hoisin sauce

1 tablespoon soy sauce

½ teaspoon chilli flakes

1 red capsicum, diced

1 green capsicum, diced

6 green onions, diced

1 head broccoli, separated into florets

1 Thinly slice the chicken breast fillets. Heat a frying pan, add the sweet chilli sauce, hoisin sauce, soy sauce and chilli flakes and stir well.

2 When the sauce begins to bubble, add the chicken fillets and stir to combine. Cook for 2 minutes, then add the vegetables and stir-fry. Cover and cook for another 3 minutes, stirring regularly. Serve with boiled rice.

Serves 4

Tangy Tenderloins

(see photograph opposite)

500g chicken tenderloins

salt and pepper

olive oil spray

200g sugar peas

400g can baby corn, drained

½ cup apricot nectar

2 tablespoons cider vinegar

2 tablespoons sweet chilli sauce

1 Flatten the tenderloins slightly and sprinkle with salt and pepper. Heat a heavy-based frying pan and spray lightly with oil spray. Add the tenderloins and cook for 2 minutes each side. Remove from the pan.

2 Add the sugar peas and stir around the pan until they brighten in colour. Add the corn.Return the chicken to the pan and toss with the vegetables. Combine the 2 sauces and vinegar. Pour over the chicken and vegetables and heat through. Pile onto serving plates. Serve immediately.

Serves 5

Chilli Tomato Chicken

3 single boneless, skinless
chicken breasts

3 tablespoons cornflour

½ teaspoon salt

¼ teaspoon five spice powder

½ cup chicken stock

2 tablespoons chilli sauce

¼ cup tomato paste

2 cloves garlic

¼ cup peanut oil

1 tablespoon finely chopped root
ginger

tomato slices

snow pea sprouts

1   Cut chicken into thin strips. Mix cornflour, salt and five spice powder together
in a plastic bag. Toss chicken in bag to coat with cornflour mixture. Mix
chicken stock, chilli sauce and tomato paste together. Crush, peel and chop
garlic.

2   Heat two tablespoons of the oil in a wok or frying pan. Stir fry a quarter of
the chicken at a time until brown and cooked. Remove from wok.

3   Drain on absorbent paper and set aside while cooking remaining batches of
chicken, adding more oil as necessary. Add garlic and ginger to wok and
stir fry for 30 seconds. Add tomato paste mixture to wok. Bring to the boil.
Return chicken to wok to heat through.

4   Serve garnished with tomato slices and snow pea sprouts.

Serves 4

Sweet and Sour Chicken

1 onion

2 sticks celery

1 carrot

½ green capsicum

432g can pineapple pieces in juice

¼ cup water

2 teaspoons ground ginger

1 tablespoon golden syrup

2 tablespoons white vinegar

½ teaspoon Tabasco sauce

2 single skinless, boneless
  chicken breasts

2 tablespoons cornflour

3 tablespoons peanut oil

1 teaspoon salt

snow pea sprouts

1 Peel onion and cut into eighths. Trim celery and string. Cut into 1cm slices on the diagonal. Peel carrot and slice finely. Remove core from capsicum and cut flesh into thin slices. Drain pineapple, reserving juice. Mix juice, water, ginger, golden syrup, vinegar and Tabasco sauce together. Cut chicken into 1cm strips. Toss in cornflour.

2 Heat oil in a wok and stir fry chicken in batches for 2 to 3 minutes or until cooked. Drain on absorbent paper. Add vegetables and pineapple to wok and stir fry for 3 minutes. Pour in pineapple juice mixture and cook for 2 minutes. Season with salt. Return chicken to wok. Bring to the boil and serve immediately, garnished with snow pea sprouts.

Serves 4

Note: There are so many sweet and sour combinations that a whole book could be devoted to this flavour match. Use this basic sweet and sour sauce mix in a recipe with chicken, fish, pork or beef, depending on what you have on hand at the time.

Chicken and Noodle Stir Fry

1 clove garlic

1 small red onion

3 bunches small bok choy

2 tablespoons oil

500g skinless, boneless chicken stir fry

2 teaspoons prepared minced ginger

150g fresh egg noodles

½ cup hot chicken stock

1 Crush, peel and finely chop garlic. Peel onion and slice finely. Wash bok choy, trim and cut into quarters lengthwise.

2 Heat oil in a wok or frying pan. Stir fry chicken, garlic, onion and ginger for 2 to 3 minutes. Add bok choy. Break up noodles and add to wok with stock.

3 Toss regularly for 3 to 4 minutes or until all the liquid has evaporated. Serve hot.

Serves 4

Note: When a recipe calls for hot stock, dissolve powdered stock or cubes in boiling water or heat stock in a jug in the microwave.

Chicken with Beans and Walnuts

2 single boneless, skinless

chicken breasts

2 teaspoons sherry

1 teaspoon soy sauce

1 teaspoon water

¼ teaspoon sugar

1 teaspoon cornflour

salt

pepper

1 teaspoon peanut oil

extra peanut oil

½ cup walnuts

200g fresh or frozen French beans

2 cloves garlic

¼ teaspoon sesame oil

1   Cut chicken into bite-sized pieces. Place chicken in a bowl with half the
    sherry, the soy sauce, water, sugar, cornflour, and salt and pepper to taste.
    Pour the measured peanut oil over and set aside for 30 minutes.

2   Heat 2 to 3cm of peanut oil in a wok or large frying pan. Add walnuts and
    stir fry for about 2 minutes, taking care they do not burn. Drain and set aside.

3   Drain oil from wok leaving about one tablespoon. Trim beans if necessary.
    Cut in half crosswise. Crush, peel and mash garlic. Heat oil and stir fry
    chicken over a high heat until it changes colour. Remove from wok and set
    aside. Reduce heat.

4   Stir fry beans for 2 minutes. Remove and set aside. Add garlic and saute
    over a low heat. Increase heat and add chicken, remaining sherry and
    beans. Stir fry for 5 to 8 minutes or until chicken is cooked. Stir in walnuts
    and sprinkle sesame oil over top. Serve immediately.

Serves 2–3

Japanese Noodles with Chicken

250g packet soba noodles

2 cooked, skinless, boneless chicken
 breasts, or about 2 cups cooked
 chicken

1 carrot

¼ telegraph cucumber

3 green onions

1 tablespoon sesame oil

2 teaspoons prepared minced ginger

DRESSING

3 tablespoons peanut oil

3 tablespoons soy sauce

½ teaspoon wasabi powder

1 Cook noodles in boiling, salted water for 3 minutes or to packet directions. Drain and rinse under cold running water to stop cooking. Cut chicken into thin strips. Peel carrot. Cut carrot and cucumber into matchstick-sized pieces. Trim green onions and slice finely.

2 Heat sesame oil in a saucepan. Add carrots and stir fry for 2 minutes. Add cucumber, green onions and ginger and stir fry for 1 minute. Toss chicken, vegetables, noodles and dressing together. Serve warm or cold.

DRESSING

1 Mix oil, soy sauce and wasabi together until combined.

Serves 4

Note: Noodles don't always have to be served hot. Try this for a spring or summer meal. It's a great way to use leftover chicken.

Chicken and Broccoli Stir-Fry

1 clove garlic

1 small onion

1 head broccoli

1 red capsicum

500g boneless, skinless chicken

1 teaspoon grated root ginger

1 tablespoon soy sauce

2 tablespoons dry sherry

1 teaspoon sugar

2 teaspoons chicken stock powder

2 teaspoons cornflour

1 Crush, peel and chop garlic. Peel onion and cut into quarters, separating layers. Cut broccoli into florets. Peel broccoli stem and cut into strips. Cut capsicum in half and remove core. Cut flesh into thin strips. Cut chicken into thin strips. Spray or grease a wok or large frying pan with oil.

2 Heat, then stir fry garlic, onion, ginger, broccoli and capsicum for 3 to 4 minutes. Remove from wok and set aside.

3 Stir fry chicken for 2 to 3 minutes or until just cooked. Mix soy sauce, sherry, sugar, chicken stock powder and cornflour together. Return broccoli mixture to wok and pour in soy mixture. Heat through and serve immediately.

Serves 4–6

Ginger Chicken

1 tablespoon cornflour

1 tablespoon soy sauce

500g chicken tenderloins

2 tablespoons grated root ginger

1 tablespoon white vinegar

1 teaspoon sugar

1 teaspoon ground ginger

½ teaspoon salt

100g snow peas

12 large spinach leaves

3 tablespoons peanut oil

pickled ginger

1   Mix cornflour and soy sauce together and toss tenderloins in this. Set aside. Mix root ginger, vinegar, sugar, ground ginger and salt together. Trim snow peas and wash spinach.

2   Heat oil in a wok or frying pan. Stir fry chicken for 2 to 3 minutes or until just cooked. Add ginger mixture, snow peas and spinach. Stir fry for 2 minutes. Serve immediately accompanied by pickled ginger.

Serves 4

Nyonya Chicken Stir-Fry

500g skinless, boneless chicken

1 stalk fresh or preserved lemon grass

3 green onions

2 tablespoon oil

1 tablespoon prepared minced ginger

1 teaspoon chilli powder

¼ cup lime juice

1 teaspoon sugar

½ cup coconut milk

1 tablespoon soy sauce

1 Cut chicken into thin strips. Trim lemon grass, slit lengthwise and chop very finely. Trim green onions and cut into 0.5cm sliced on the diagonal.

2 Heat oil in a wok and stir-fry chicken in small batches. Remove each batch from wok and set aside. Stir-fry lemon grass, green onions and ginger for 2 minutes. Add chilli and cook for 1 minute or until chilli smells fragrant. Add lime juice, sugar, coconut milk and soy sauce to wok. Return chicken to wok. Heat and serve.

Serves 4

Chicken Stroganoff Stir-Fry

350g chicken tenderloins or stir-fry

1 tablespoon oil

220g can mushrooms in sauce

¼ cup onion stock

1 teaspoon paprika

½ cup low-fat sour cream

2 tablespoons chopped fresh parsley to garnish

1 Cut tenderloins in half lengthwise.

2 Heat oil in a wok or heavy-based frying pan. Stir-fry chicken for 4 minutes or until just cooked. Add mushrooms in sauce, stock and paprika. Bring to the boil. Stir in sour cream. Simmer for 2 minutes.

3 Serve garnished with parsley.

Serves 2–3

Note: Tenderloins are so quick to cook and don't need any preparation. The tenderloin is the piece between the chicken breast and the bone.

grills

Chicken with Lemon Coriander Couscous

(see photograph on page 72)

4 wooden skewers

4 large skinless boneless chicken breasts, cut into 25mm cubes

1 tablespoon olive oil

1 clove garlic, crushed

1 teaspoon each of ground coriander, ginger and cinnamon

pinch of cayenne pepper

½ teaspoon salt

juice of 1½ lemons

2 cups couscous

2 tablespoon butter

2 tablespoon chopped fresh coriander, plus extra leaves to garnish

6 tablespoon pitted black olives, chopped

black pepper

lemon wedges to serve

1 Soak 4 wooden skewers in water for at least 10 minutes. Toss the chicken with the oil, garlic, ground spices, cayenne, salt, and 1 tablespoon of lemon juice until the pieces are evenly coated.

2 Preheat the grill to high. Thread the chicken onto the skewers and grill for 8–10 minutes, turning occasionally, until slightly charred, cooked through and tender. Keep warm.

3 Meanwhile, prepare the couscous according to packet instructions, then fluff it up with a fork. Stir the butter, remaining lemon juice, coriander, and olives into couscous and season. Transfer to serving plates, top with chicken, and drizzle over any pan juices. Serve with the lemon wedges and garnish with coriander.

Serves 4

Street Vendor Barbecued Chicken Drums

(see photograph opposite)

4 cloves garlic

1 teaspoon salt

2 teaspoons prepared chopped lemongrass

¼ teaspoon chilli powder

1 teaspoon turmeric

1 teaspoon ground coriander

8 chicken drumsticks

mango chutney

1 Crush, peel and finely chop garlic. Mix garlic, salt, lemongrass, chilli powder, turmeric and coriander together in a plastic bag. Add chicken drumsticks and toss to coat. Refrigerate mixture overnight if possible, or cook straightaway if necessary.

2 Grill or barbecue chicken for 30 to 35 minutes or until juices run clear when tested. Serve with mango chutney.

Serves 4

Malaysian Grilled Chicken

4 skinless chicken breasts on the bone

2 teaspoons cornflour blended with
 2 tablespoons water

cucumber slices

red pepper strips, optional

SPICY ORIENTAL MARINADE

1 red onion, quartered

2 cloves garlic, chopped

1 tablespoon grated fresh ginger

1 tablespoon ground coriander

1 tablespoon palm sugar, crumbled, or
 brown sugar

1 teaspoon Chinese five spice powder

¼ cup rice wine (mirin)

¼ cup orange or lime juice

1 tablespoon reduced-salt thick dark
 soy sauce

1 To make the marinade, place the onion and garlic in a food processor. Process to finely chop. Transfer to a bowl. Add the ginger, coriander, sugar, five spice powder, wine, orange juice and soy sauce. Mix to combine.

2 Place the chicken in a shallow glass or ceramic dish. Pour over the marinade. Turn to coat. Cover. Marinate in the refrigerator overnight. Transfer the chicken and marinade to a large non-stick frying pan.

3 Place the pan over a medium heat. Bring to the boil. Reduce the heat. Simmer for 15–20 minutes or until chicken is just tender; take care not to overcook. Using a slotted spoon, remove the chicken from the cooking liquid. Place in a clean dish. Cover. Refrigerate until ready to barbecue or stir-fry. Reserve the marinade.

4 Preheat the barbecue to a medium heat. Cook the chicken on barbecue grill for 5 minutes each side or until richly coloured and heated through. Alternatively, heat a little oil in a wok over a high heat. Add the chicken. Stir-fry for 3–4 minutes or until heated through.

5 Place the reserved marinade and the cornflour mixture in a small saucepan over a medium heat. Cook, stirring constantly, for 4–5 minutes or until the sauce boils and thickens.

6 To serve, spoon the sauce over the chicken and accompany with cucumber, red pepper and steamed rice.

Serves 4

Cajun Chicken Brochettes

3 large skinless boneless chicken breasts, cut into 25mm pieces

salt and black pepper

olive oil for brushing

MARINADE

3 tablespoons Dijon mustard

3 tablespoons clear honey

1 tablespoon olive oil

2 tablespoons tomato sauce

½ teaspoon Tabasco

1 clove garlic, crushed

½ teaspoon dried thyme

3 basil leaves, finely chopped, plus extra leaves to garnish

6 skewers

PEACH SALSA

3 peaches, fresh or canned

⅓ cup natural yoghurt

1 teaspoon lemon juice

1. To make the marinade, mix the mustard, honey, oil, tomato sauce, Tabasco, garlic, thyme and basil in a shallow, non-metallic dish that is large enough to hold 6 skewers. If using wooden skewers, soak them in water for 10 minutes.

2. Season the chicken, with a little salt and pepper, then thread them onto the skewers. Add to the marinade and turn until coated. Cover and place in the refrigerator for 1 hour, stirring occasionally.

3. Meanwhile, make the peach salsa. If using fresh peaches, put them into a bowl, cover with boiling water and leave for 30 seconds. Peel off the skins, remove the stones and chop. If using canned peaches, chop the flesh. Mix the peaches with the yoghurt and lemon juice, season with black pepper, cover and refrigerate until needed.

4. Preheat the grill to high and brush the rack with oil. Place the brochettes on the grill rack, brush with half the marinade and grill for 6 minutes. Turn them over, brush with the rest of the marinade and grill for a further 2–3 minutes, until the chicken is tender and cooked through. Serve with the salsa, garnished with basil.

Serves 6

Note: Tender chunks of chicken in a piquant marinade are set off by a peach and yoghurt salsa. You'll love it so much you may want to double the quantities and serve it as a main course.

Southern Barbecued Chicken

1¾ kg fresh chicken, cut into pieces

SOUTHERN BARBECUE SAUCE

1⅓ cups tomato purée

1 cup cider vinegar

½ cup rapeseed oil

⅓ cup Worcestershire sauce

½ cup brown sugar

¼ cup Golden syrup or molasses

2 tablespoons French mustard

3 cloves garlic, ground

¼ cup lemon juice

1 Prepare the Southern Barbecue Sauce in advance. Place all the ingredients into a stainless steel saucepan and stir to combine. Bring to a simmer and continue to simmer over low heat for 15–20 minutes, stirring regularly to prevent catching. Stand for 1 hour to cook and to allow the flavours to blend. Store in jars or bottles in the refrigerator (if not used immediately).

2 Cut the chicken into pieces. As a 1¾ kg chicken is a large bird, the breast can be cut into 3–4 pieces each side. Heat the barbecue to moderate and oil the grill plate. Lightly sear the chicken pieces on all sides over a direct heat, about 4 minutes each side. Lift the chicken onto a plate.

3 Place 1½ cups of the sauce into a bowl and place by the barbecue. Place a sheet of baking paper over the grill bars and prick at intervals between the runs to allow ventilation. Replace the chicken onto the baking paper and brush well with the sauce.

4 Close the lid and cook for 10 minutes, then lift the lid, brush with sauce, turn the chicken, brush the underside with sauce, close lid and cook for 10 minutes. Repeat this process every 10 minutes for a total of 4–5 times or 40–50 minutes until the chicken is rich brown in colour and cooked through. If the chicken is cooking too quickly, reduce the heat by turning down the gas or raking the coals to the sides. Heat the extra sauce in a small saucepan on the barbecue.

5 Serve the chicken with the hot sauce and jacket potatoes cooked on the barbecue with the chicken. Accompany with a salad.

Serves 6–8

Grilled Sesame Chicken with Ginger Rice

500g skinless chicken breast or thigh
fillets or tenderloin, trimmed of
visible fat

SOY AND HONEY MARINADE

1 tablespoon sesame seeds, toasted

1 tablespoon rice wine (mirin) or sherry

2 teaspoons honey or plum sauce

2 teaspoons reduced-salt soy sauce

2 teaspoons oyster sauce

1 teaspoon sesame oil

GINGER RICE

1 tablespoon finely chopped fresh
ginger

1 teaspoon sesame oil

1 cup short or medium grain rice,
rinsed and drained

1½ cups ginger beer

1 tablespoon diced pickled or
preserved ginger

1 tablespoon finely chopped spring
onion, optional

1 To make the marinade, place the sesame seeds, wine, sauces and sesame
oil in a non-reactive bowl. Mix to combine.

2 Cut the chicken into large pieces. Add to the marinade. Toss to coat. Cover.
Marinate in the refrigerator for at least 1 hour.

3 To make the rice, place fresh ginger and sesame oil in a large saucepan
over a low heat. Cook, stirring occasionally, for 5 minutes. Add the rice.
Cook, stirring, for 2 minutes. Stir in the ginger beer and pickled ginger. Bring
to the boil. Reduce the heat. Cover. Steam for 10–15 minutes or until the
liquid is absorbed and the rice is cooked. Stir in spring onion.

4 Meanwhile, preheat the grill or barbecue to a medium heat. Drain the
chicken. Cook under the grill or on the barbecue, brushing occasionally with
marinade, for 6–7 minutes or until cooked through and slightly crispy on the
outside. The chicken is cooked when the juices run clear when pressed with
a fork. Serve chicken with the Ginger Rice and steamed Chinese greens.

Serves 4

Chicken Kebabs with Couscous

4 chicken breast fillets (skin off) cut into
24 pieces

1 yellow and 1 red pepper, deseeded
and cut into 8 pieces

juice of 1 lemon

2 garlic cloves, crushed

2 tablespoons extra virgin olive oil

1 tablespoon chopped fresh coriander

SAUCE

⅗ cup natural yoghurt

1 tablespoon lemon juice

finely grated rind of ½ lemon

sea salt and freshly ground black
pepper

4 large wooden skewers

COUSCOUS

250g couscous

30g butter

4 spring onions, finely chopped

3 tablespoons chopped fresh coriander

1 Place the chicken and peppers in a non-metallic bowl, add the lemon juice, garlic, olive oil and coriander and mix. Cover and leave to marinate for at least 1 hour. Meanwhile, combine all the ingredients for the sauce. Season with salt and pepper and leave to chill. Soak four large wooden skewers in water for about 10 minutes.

2 Preheat the grill to high. Thread the chicken and capsicums onto the skewers and grill for 10–12 minutes, turning occasionally, until the chicken is slightly charred, cooked through and tender. Keep warm.

3 Meanwhile, prepare the couscous according to packet instructions, then fluff up with a fork. Melt the butter in a small saucepan and fry the spring onions for about 2 minutes. Add the spring onions with 3 tablespoons of coriander and plenty of seasoning to the couscous and mix well. Serve the couscous on plates, with the kebabs on top, then drizzle with the yoghurt sauce.

Serves 4

Note: The lemony marinade infuses the chicken and capsicum with its lovely flavour and tenderises the meat. Marinate overnight if possible.

Chicken Kebabs with Yoghurt and Lemon Sauce

24 wooden satay skewers

1 cup plain yoghurt

2 cloves garlic, crushed

1½ teaspoon paprika, ground

1½ teaspoons cumin seeds

4 tablespoons lemon juice

2 tablespoons parsley, chopped

2 teaspoons oregano, chopped

freshly ground black pepper

oil for cooking

6 chicken thigh fillets, cubed

1 Soak the wooden satay skewers in cold water for 30 minutes.

2 Place the yoghurt, garlic, paprika, cumin seeds, lemon juice, parsley, oregano and pepper and mix until combined.

3 Place the chicken on the satay and brush over skewers with half the mixture. Leave to marinate in refrigerator for 2–3 hours.

4 Heat the oil on the barbecue (or chargrill pan), add the chicken kebabs and cook 4–5 minutes each side.

5 Serve with the remaining marinade mixture.

Serves 4

Spicy Marinated Chicken

1 tablespoon ground coriander

1 teaspoon ground cumin

2 teaspoons ground ginger

2 cloves garlic

2 teaspoons prepared minced ginger

¼ cup white wine vinegar

8 chicken drumsticks

1   Mix coriander, cumin and ground ginger together. Crush, peel and chop garlic. Add to spices with the minced ginger and vinegar. Mix well. Remove skin from chicken drumsticks and discard. Marinate chicken in spicy mixture for a minimum of an hour.

2   Grill or barbecue chicken for about 25 minutes or until juices run clear when tested. Serve with sweet chilli sauce.

Serves 4

Note: Use prepared crushed garlic if you wish. I prefer to use fresh garlic whenever possible as the processing tends to lose some of the lovely fresh "top notes" from the garlic.

roasts
and bakes

Vindaloo Chicken Nuggets

(see photograph on page 88)

1 kg chicken thigh fillets

salt and pepper

1 tablespoon lemon juice

3 tablespoons vindaloo curry paste

1 cup plain flour

2 eggs, beaten

1½ cups dried breadcrumbs

vegetable oil spray

1 Cut each fillet into 4 pieces. Place in a bowl, sprinkle lightly with salt and pepper then pour over the lemon juice. Toss with a spoon to mix through. Rub the curry paste well into each piece with your fingers. Cover and refrigerate for 2 hours or more.

2 Coat the fillets with flour, egg and breadcrumbs as for schnitzels. Lightly spray a large flat tray with canola oil spray and place on the nuggets. Lightly spray the surface of the nuggets. Cook in a preheated oven 180°C for 15–18 minutes.

Serves 6

Roasted Herby Chicken with Pears

(see photograph opposite)

juice of 2 lemons

salt and black pepper

12 chicken drumsticks, skinned

6 firm pears, peeled, halved, cored and cut crossways into 1cm slices

¾ cup white wine

1 tablespoon chopped fresh thyme or

1 teaspoon dried thyme

1 tablespoon chopped fresh tarragon

1 tablespoon chopped fresh rosemary

1 Mix together the lemon juice and seasoning. Put the drumsticks into a shallow, non-metallic bowl, pour over the seasoned lemon juice and rub into the skin with your fingertips. Cover and marinate in the fridge for 30 minutes.

2 Meanwhile, preheat the oven to 200°C. Arrange the pears in a deep ovenproof dish, then top with the chicken and pour over the marinating juices. Pour over the wine and sprinkle with the thyme, tarragon and rosemary. Cover the dish with foil.

3 Cook for 1 hour, basting 1–2 times, until the chicken is tender. Remove the foil and increase the oven temperature to 230°C. Cook for a further 10 minutes or until the chicken is cooked through and the skin has browned. Leave it to rest, covered, for 10 minutes before serving.

Serves 6

Note: Sweet pears, chicken and fragrant herbs are a magical combination. The tarragon and rosemary add their flavour without overpowering the chicken.

Crunchy Drumsticks

1 kg chicken drumsticks

2 tablespoons curry paste

2 cups vinegar-flavoured corn chips or crisps

boiled rice or salad

mild chutney for serving

1 Rinse the drumsticks and pat dry. With your fingers, rub the curry paste well into the skin of the drumsticks.

2 Crush the corn chips or crisps and press onto the drumsticks. Place the drumsticks on a rack over a shallow baking tray. Bake at 180°C in a preheated oven for 35–40 minutes.

3 Serve hot with boiled rice and some chutney on the side. May also be served cold with salad.

Serves 4

Note: A shallow dish is recommended as it aids the crisping process.

Easy Apricot and Mango Chicken Loaf

750g minced chicken meat

60g fresh breadcrumbs

90g spring onions, chopped

1 tablespoon finely

chopped parsley

2 tablespoons dried apricots

1 tablespoon mango chutney

1 egg

1 teaspoon salt

¼ teaspoon pepper

vegetable oil for greasing

1 Place the minced chicken in a large bowl. Add all remaining ingredients. With your hand, mix and knead the mixture for 2–3 minutes to combine ingredients well and to give a fine texture.

2 Grease a 22 x 8 x 5cm loaf tin with oil. Pour in the mixture. Place in a preheated oven 180°C for 50–55 minutes. Rest in tin for 10 minutes before serving.

3 Serve hot with vegetable accompaniments or cold with salad.

Serves 6

Apricot Glazed Chicken with Savoury Stuffing

1⅓ kg fresh chicken

1 tablespoon soy sauce

½ lemon

APRICOT DIPPING SAUCE

½ cup apricot jam

1 tablespoon soy sauce

1 tablespoon lemon juice

2 tablespoons white vinegar

1 tablespoon water

EASY STUFFING

4 rashers bacon, chopped

1 large onion, finely chopped

1½ cups long-grain rice, rinsed

3 cups boiling water

2 teaspoons soy sauce

2 teaspoons mixed dried herbs

2 tablespoons chopped parsley

1 tablespoon flour, for gravy

1 To make the sauce, mix all the sauce ingredients together and heat gently while stirring.

2 Prepare the chicken for roasting. Mix together the Apricot Dipping Sauce and soy sauce, brush over the chicken and inside the cavity. Place the lemon half in the cavity. Place the chicken on an adjustable rack, breast-side down. Add a cup of water to the dish and cook in a preheated oven 180°C for 40 minutes. Brush again with sauce and turn breast-side up, brush with sauce and cook for 40–50 minutes more, until cooked when tested.

3 When the chicken is placed in the oven, prepare the stuffing. Place all ingredients in a lidded casserole dish and place on a shelf in the oven under the chicken. Cook for 40 minutes then remove from oven and stand covered for 10 minutes. When the chicken is cooked, remove from the dish and cover with foil to rest. Skim the fat from roasting the pan and add about 1 cup of water to dissolve any cooked-on pan juices. Pour into a small saucepan. Add 1 tablespoon of flour blended with a little water and stir until it thickens and boils.

4 Carve the chicken and serve with the stuffing, gravy and vegetable accompaniments.

Serves 4

Note: To test for doneness, pierce the thickest part of breast and thigh with a skewer. If the juices run clear, the chicken is cooked. If the juices have a pink tinge, more cooking is needed.

Quick Chicken Lasagne

500g chicken thigh fillets

salt and pepper

1½ cups packaged tomato salsa of
choice

250g instant lasagne sheets

90g mushrooms, sliced

TOPPING

250g ricotta cheese

200ml plain yoghurt

2 tablespoons grated Romano or
Parmesan cheese

pinch nutmeg

2 eggs, lightly beaten

1   Place the fillets between 2 pieces of plastic wrap and pound with a meat mallet until thin. Season with salt and pepper.

2   Grease a baking dish or lasagne dish with oil. Spread a thin layer of sauce in the base of the dish. Dip 3–4 lasagne sheets into a dish of water and place to cover base. Spread them generously with sauce. Place the thigh fillets over the sauce in a single layer and cover with mushrooms. Wet 4 lasagne sheets and layer over the mushrooms. Spread the remaining sauce over the lasagne sheets.

3   Mix together all the topping ingredients and spread over the lasagne. Grate a little extra Parmesan over the surface and dot with small flecks of butter. Place in preheated oven 180°C for 35–40 minutes.

4   Stand for 10 minutes before serving for the lasagne sheets to re-absorb loose moisture.

Serves 6

Oven Baked Chicken Schnitzels

1 kg chicken breast fillets (skin off)

salt and pepper

juice of 1 lemon

2 tablespoons sweet chilli sauce

¾ cup flour

2 eggs

1½ cups dried breadcrumbs

olive oil spray

1   Place each fillet between 2 pieces of plastic wrap and flatten to an even thinness with the side of a meat mallet or rolling pin. Place on a platter. Mix the salt, pepper, lemon juice and chilli sauce together and pour over the chicken. Cover and refrigerate for 20 minutes.

2   Spread the flour onto a sheet of kitchen paper. Beat the eggs with one tablespoon of water and place in a shallow tray or dish. Spread the breadcrumbs onto a sheet of kitchen paper. Coat each side of the chicken fillets in flour (shake off excess) then egg and press into the breadcrumbs to coat both sides. Place on a flat surface in a single layer. Lightly spray the schnitzels with oil spray.

3   Place them oiled side down on a rack over an oven tray (a cake-rack is suitable). Lightly spray the top-side with oil spray. Place in a preheated oven 180°C and cook for 8 minutes, turn with tongs and cook for 8 minutes more.

4   Serve with vegetable accompaniments or a salad.

Serves 5–6

Tandoori Chicken

2 x 1 kg fresh chickens

3 tablespoons tandoori curry paste

200g tub natural yoghurt

2 tablespoons lemon juice

2 tablespoons melted butter

lettuce, onion rings, tomato and lemon
  for serving

1 Rinse chickens inside and out and pat dry with paper towels. Make deep gashes in the thighs and on each side of breast. Pin back the wings.

2 Mix the tandoori paste, yoghurt, lemon juice and melted butter together. Place the chickens in a stainless steel or other non-metal dish and spread the mixture all over, rubbing well into the gashes. Cover and refrigerate for 12 or more hours. Place chickens on a roasting rack in a baking dish and spoon any remaining marinade over chickens.

3 Place in a preheated oven 190°C and cook for 1 hour. Baste with the pan juices during cooking. When cooked cover with foil and rest for 10 minutes before serving. Arrange crisp lettuce leaves on a large platter and cover with onion rings. Cut chicken into portions and place on the platter. Garnish with tomato wedges and lemon slices.

Serves 8–10

Satay Wings for a Crowd

1 kg chicken wings

¾ cup spicy satay sauce

SPICY SATAY SAUCE

¾ cup peanut butter

¾ cup water

2 tablespoons brown sugar

⅛ teaspoon chilli powder, or to taste

1 tablespoon soy sauce

1 tablespoon grated onion

2 tablespoons toasted sesame seeds

bamboo skewers, soaked

1 Rinse the wings and pat dry with a paper towel. Cut off each wing tip and discard. Cut through the next joint to make two pieces. Place all the wings in a bowl and stir through the satay sauce. Cover and marinate for 2 hours or more in the refrigerator; may be left overnight.

2 Arrange the wing pieces underside upward on a rack over a shallow dish or tray lined with foil. Place in a preheated oven 180°C for 15 minutes. Brush some of the remaining marinade on wing pieces, then turn them over and brush again. Cook for 20 minutes more. Brush with marinade, increase the heat to 200°C and cook for about 5 minutes more.

3 Remove from the oven. Brush with 1 tablespoon of fresh satay sauce (do not use remaining marinade), to intensify the flavour.

4 Arrange on platter and serve hot as finger food.

5 To make the sauce, mix all ingredients in a saucepan, heat to a simmer. Keep on the heat for 5 minutes and allow to cool.

Makes 32

Roast Chicken with Basil and Red Onion

(see photograph opposite)

1⅓ kg chicken

15g fresh basil

½ cup extra virgin olive oil

juice of ½ lemon

sea salt and freshly ground

black pepper

ONIONS

4 medium red onions

grated zest of ½ lemon

1 garlic clove, crushed

1   Preheat the oven to 190°C. Place the chicken in a roasting tray. Gently work the skin away from the flesh with your fingers and tuck 6–7 basil leaves under the breast skin of the chicken. Place the remaining basil in a liquidiser with the olive oil, lemon juice and seasoning and blend until smooth. Brush the chicken with half the basil oil and cook for 40 minutes.

2   Meanwhile, prepare the onions. Peel them and slice off the root bottom to give a flat base. Make 4 cuts, in a criss-cross shape, across the top of each onion, coming only halfway down, so the onions open slightly. Combine the lemon zest with the garlic and sprinkle this over the onions.

3   Add the onions to the chicken in the tray and brush well with some of the basil oil. Brush the remaining oil over the chicken and cook for a further 40 minutes or until cooked through. Cover and allow the chicken to rest for 10 minutes before carving.

Serves 4

Note: Tucking basil leaves under the skin adds great flavour. The red onions are the perfect accompaniment.

Cajun Chicken with Papaya Salsa

(see photograph page 89)

4 boneless chicken breast fillets, skinned and trimmed of all visible fat

2 cloves garlic, crushed

1 tablespoon onion salt

1 tablespoon ground white pepper

1 tablespoon cracked black pepper

2 teaspoons cayenne pepper

1 tablespoon paprika

1 tablespoon dried mixed herbs

PAPAYA SALSA

1 small papaya, diced

1 cucumber, diced

2 tablespoons mint leaves

2 tablespoons low-fat natural yoghurt

2 tablespoons lime juice

1   Rub the chicken with crushed garlic. Place onion salt, white pepper, black pepper, cayenne pepper, paprika and mixed herbs in a bowl and mix to combine.

2   Rub spice mixture over the chicken, place on a non-stick baking tray and bake at 180°C for 25–30 minutes or until chicken is tender. Cover and stand for 5 minutes before serving.

PAPAYA SALSA

1   Place pawpaw, cucumber, mint, yoghurt and lime juice in a bowl and mix to combine. Serve with the chicken.

Serves 4

Note: After rubbing spice mixture onto the chicken, wash your hands and do not touch your face or lips as the cayenne pepper causes burning.

Asian Marinated Chicken Drumsticks

12 large chicken drumsticks

½ cup hoisin sauce

3 tablespoons corn or golden syrup

1 tablespoon lemon juice

1 tablespoon sunflower oil

2 cloves garlic, crushed

4 spring onions, thinly sliced on the
  diagonal

4 baby bok choy, halved

steamed rice, to serve

1   Remove the skin from the drumsticks and discard any excess fat. Make
    2–3 deep slashes in the fleshy part of the chicken.

2   Put the sauce, syrup, lemon juice, oil and garlic in a large bowl and mix to
    combine. Coat the drumsticks with the mixture, cover and marinate in the
    refrigerator for 1 hour or overnight if you have time.

3   Preheat the oven to 200°C. Line a baking tray with non stick paper. Put the
    drumsticks on the paper and roast for 40 minutes or until the juices run clear
    when tested with a skewer. Sprinkle the drumsticks with the spring onions.

4   Steam the bok choy in a bamboo steamer over a wok of simmering water,
    making sure the base of the steamer does not touch the water. Serve the
    chicken on top of the steamed bok choy with steamed rice on the side.

Serves 4

Roasted Herb Stuffed Chicken

4 chicken breasts, skin on

2 tablespoons thick natural yoghurt

1 clove garlic, crushed

1 teaspoon olive oil

2 tablespoons mint, finely chopped

2 tablespoons Italian parsley, finely chopped

2 tablespoons oregano, finely chopped

2 tablespoons thyme, finely chopped

2 tablespoons fennel, finely chopped

2 green onions, finely chopped

salt and finely ground black pepper

1   In a small bowl combine all ingredients except the chicken and mix well.

2   Using your fingertips, scoop up quarter of the mixture and gently push it under the skin of the chicken. Run your fingers over the skin to smooth the stuffing out. Repeat with the remaining pieces. Cover and refrigerate for 1½ hours.

3   Pre-heat the oven to 180°C, place the chicken on a roasting rack and cook for 15–17 minutes. When the juices run clear, the chicken is cooked.

Serves 4–6

Note: All the herbs need to be very finely chopped.

Oven Baked Parmesan Chicken

30g fresh breadcrumbs, made from 1
  slice white loaf, crusts removed

90g Parmesan, finely grated

2 spring onions, finely chopped

finely grated zest and juice of ½ lemon

60g butter, melted

sea salt and freshly ground black
  pepper

4 skinless chicken breast fillets

2 tablespoons chopped fresh parsley

1 Preheat the oven to 190°C. Mix the breadcrumbs, Parmesan, spring onions, lemon zest, butter and seasoning together in a small bowl. Divide the mixture between the chicken breasts and, using a fork, press the mixture down on top, to form an even coat.

2 Transfer the chicken breasts to a shallow roasting tin and bake for 20 minutes. Remove the chicken from the roasting tin and keep warm. Add the lemon juice and parsley to the buttery juices in the tin and mix well. Pour these juices over the chicken and serve straight away.

Serves 4

Note: Cooked in a coat of Parmesan and breadcrumbs, the chicken breasts keep moist and succulent. Serve with new potatoes and a green vegetable or salad.

Chicken and Prune Roll

2 rashers of bacon, trimmed of fat and finely chopped

1 medium onion, finely chopped

10 pitted prunes

500g minced chicken meat

2 tablespoons dried breadcrumbs

½ teaspoon each salt and pepper

1 teaspoon cumin

1 egg, lightly beaten

1 sheet frozen puff pastry

1 tablespoon milk

2 teaspoons poppy seeds

1 Place the bacon and onion in a small heated pan and cook while stirring for 1 minute. Chop 5 prunes finely; add to the minced chicken along with the breadcrumbs, seasonings, egg and bacon/onion mixture. Mix well to distribute the ingredients.

2 Line a flat oven tray with a sheet of baking paper or foil and place a sheet of thawed puff pastry onto the tray. Spoon ½ of the meat mixture along the centre of the sheet in an even strip about 3in wide and to the edge of the pastry at both ends. Arrange the 5 remaining whole prunes along the centre then cover with the remaining minced chicken and smooth to even thickness.

3 Brush the back strip of pastry with water, lift the front pastry over the meat and lift the back pastry to overlap the front. Press lightly along the seam to seal. Lift the paper and turn the meat, roll over to rest on the seam join, then pull the paper to bring it into the centre of the tray. Trim off any paper overhang. Glaze the roll with milk and sprinkle with poppy seeds.

4 Bake at 200°C in a preheated hot oven for 15 minutes then turn oven down to 180°C and continue cooking for 25 minutes until golden. Serve with vegetable accompaniments

Serves 6–8

Chicken Focaccia with Marinated Vegetables

500g chicken breast fillets (skin off)

1 clove garlic, crushed

salt and pepper

1 tablespoon lemon juice

2 teaspoons olive oil

6 portions of focaccia bread (individual or slab)

1 tablespoon olive oil extra

6 slices marinated roasted aubergine

90g marinated mushrooms

6 slices marinated roasted red pepper

1 Trim the breast fillets. Place in a glass dish and add garlic, seasonings, lemon juice and oil. Cover and marinate for 30 minutes in the refrigerator. Heat a non-stick pan or greased griddle-plate, sear the fillets 1 minute each side, then cook for 3 minutes each side or until cooked through. When cooked, cut into diagonal slices. Keep hot.

2 Cut the focaccia slab into serving portions and split through the centre. Split the individual breads if using. Brush cut surfaces with olive oil.

3 Place a slice of aubergine on each base, arrange the chicken slices on top and cover with mushrooms and pepper. Replace the top slices. Place in a moderate oven (160°C) for 10 minutes. Serve hot with marinated vegetables as a light meal.

Makes 5 sandwiches

Spatchcock in Vine Leaves

2 x no. 4 spatchcocks, halved

3 tablespoons liquid honey

3 tablespoons olive oil

3 tablespoons orange juice

2 teaspoons lemon thyme, finely chopped

½ cup white wine

10 vine leaves

1 Rinse out the spatchcocks, and pat dry. Combine the honey, oil, juice, thyme and wine. Place the spatchcocks in a bowl and pour half the liquid over them. Cover and refrigerate, turning over 1–2 times over night.

2 Pre-heat the oven to 180°C.

3 Wrap the spatchcocks in vine leaves and secure with skewers. Bake in a roasting dish for 25–30 minutes. Remove the leaves, and return the spatchcocks to the oven for 10 minutes (or until cooked and brown).

4 Remove the skewers, and place the spatchcocks on their leaves.

5 Heat the remaining marinade in a pan and pour it over the spatchcocks before serving.

Serves 2

Chicken with Ricotta, Rocket and Roasted Red Pepper

200g fresh ricotta

1 cup rocket, roughly chopped

¼ cup pinenuts, toasted

½ red pepper, roasted and finely chopped

freshly ground pepper and salt

4 chicken breasts, skin on (each 170g–200g)

4 tablespoon butter

1 cup chicken stock

1 Preheat the oven to 200°C.

2 Combine the ricotta, rocket, pinenuts, capsicum and pepper and salt in a small bowl and mix together until smooth.

3 Place 1–2 tablespoons of ricotta mixture under the skin of each chicken breast. Lightly grease a baking dish. Place the chicken breasts in the dish, sprinkle with pepper and salt, place 1 teaspoon of butter on each breast and pour the stock around the chicken. Bake, for 20–25 minutes.

4 Serve the chicken with pan-juices and an rocket salad.

Serves 4

index

Apple, Chicken and Mushroom Casserole — 49

Apricot Glazed Chicken with Savoury Stuffing — 94

Asian Chicken and Kaffir Lime Salad — 28

Asian Marinated Chicken Drumsticks — 102

Bread Soup with Garlic and Eggs — 12

Cajun Chicken Brochettes — 78

Cajun Chicken with Papaya Salsa — 100

Chicken and Almond Triangles — 18

Chicken and Apricot Tagine — 48

Chicken and Broccoli Stir-Fry — 68

Chicken and Endive Salad with Creamy Dressing — 41

Chicken and Leek Soup with Herb Dumplings — 16

Chicken and Noodle Stir Fry — 64

Chicken and Papaya Salad — 37

Chicken and Prune Roll — 106

Chicken Breasts with Shiitake Mushrooms — 54

Chicken Caesar Salad — 30

Chicken Focaccia with Marinated Vegetables — 107

Chicken Kebabs with Couscous — 84

Chicken Kebabs with Yoghurt and Lemon Sauce — 86

Chicken Paprika — 51

Chicken Rolls with an Indonesian Flavour — 56

Chicken Rolls with Orange Currant Sauce — 23

Chicken Stroganoff Stir-Fry — 71

Chicken Waldorf — 26

Chicken Wings Moroccan Style — 50

Chicken with Beans and Walnuts — 65

Chicken with Lemon Coriander Couscous — 74

Chicken with Ricotta, Rocket and Roasted Red Pepper — 109

Chilli Tomato Chicken — 62

Crunchy Chicken and Potato Salad — 40

Crunchy Drumsticks — 92

Curried Chicken Salad — 32

Date and Lemon Chicken Casserole — 44

Easy Apricot and Mango Chicken Loaf — 93

Easy Chicken Stir Fry — 60

Festive Chicken Salad — 38

Ginger Chicken — 69

Grilled Sesame Chicken with Ginger Rice — 82

Hawaiian Poached Chicken — 44

Italian Chicken in a Pan — 55

Japanese Noodles with Chicken — 66

Lavash Rolls — 22

Lentil Chicken Marsala Casserole — 47

Make a Meal of Chicken Soup — 14

Malaysian Grilled Chicken — 76

Marinated Chicken Salad — 36

No-Fuss Chicken Party Sticks — 21

Nyonya Chicken Stir Fry — 70

Old-Fashioned Chicken and Vegetable Soup — 15

Oven Baked Chicken Schnitzels — 97

Oven Baked Parmesan Chicken — 104

Party Avocado and Chicken Salad — 29

Quick Chicken Lasagne — 96

Risotto of Indian Spiced Chicken with Chickpeas — 52

Roast Chicken with Basil and Red Onion	100
Roasted Herb Stuffed Chicken	103
Roasted Herby Chicken with Pears	90
Satay Wings for a Crowd	99
Southern Barbecued Chicken	80
Spatchcock in Vine Leaves	108
Spicy Chicken Burritos	20
Spicy Chicken Soup (Soto Ayam)	12
Spicy Marinated Chicken	87
Street Vendor Barbecued Chicken Drums	74
Sweet and Sour Chicken	63
Tandoori Chicken	98
Tandoori Chicken Pockets	46
Tangy Tenderloins	60
Tossed Greens and Chicken with Blue Cheese Dressing	26
Tropical Chicken Salad	33
Vindaloo Chicken Nuggets	90
Warm Salad of Mustard-Glazed Chicken with Red Wine Vinaigrette	34